Cake
Baking
& The
Creative
Process
Too

MORE Recipes for Imagination
A Guide & Resource for Educators

Judi Hofmeister

BALBOA
PRESS
A DIVISION OF HAY HOUSE

Balboa Press books may be ordered through booksellers or by contacting:

Balboa Press
A Division of Hay House
1663 Liberty Drive
Bloomington, IN 47403
www.balboapress.com
1 (877) 407-4847

Because of the dynamic nature of the Internet, any web addresses or links contained in this book may have changed since publication and may no longer be valid. The views expressed in this work are solely those of the author and do not necessarily reflect the views of the publisher, and the publisher hereby disclaims any responsibility for them.

The author of this book does not dispense medical advice or prescribe the use of any technique as a form of treatment for physical, emotional, or medical problems without the advice of a physician, either directly or indirectly. The intent of the author is only to offer information of a general nature to help you in your quest for emotional and spiritual well-being. In the event you use any of the information in this book for yourself, which is your constitutional right, the author and the publisher assume no responsibility for your actions.

Any people depicted in stock imagery provided by Getty Images are models, and such images are being used for illustrative purposes only. Certain stock imagery ° Getty Images.

Print information available on the last page.

ISBN: 978-1-4525-9004-2 (sc)
ISBN: 978-1-4525-9005-9 (e)

Library of Congress Control Number: 2014900467

Balboa Press rev. date: 04/03/2019

When I am … completely myself, entirely alone, and of good cheer … my ideas flow best and most abundantly. … It soon occurs to me, how I may turn this or that morsel to account, so as to make a good dish of it.—Mozart

Creativity is intelligence having fun.—Einstein

The universe lies before you on the floor, in the air, in the mysterious bodies of your dancers, in your mind.—Agnes De Mille

Without wonder and insight acting is just a trade. With it, it becomes creation.—Bette Davis

Nothing is impossible, the word itself says "I'm Possible!"—Audrey Hepburn

CONTENTS

FOREWORD

by Denina Brown, PhD

I have a secret for you. Judi Hofmeister is not a famous chef or even a cook. What she is, is a master of the metaphor and a magician when it comes to actively engaging students in the learning process. This book captures some of the entry points Judi has discovered for students in the search for his/her personal and vibrant creative process. Warm-up, anticipatory set, energizer, or any other new term to describe the vibrant process of gaining a student's attention and focusing it on higher order thinking and reasoning can only start when both teacher and student prepare to create. Judi helps everyone see the need for and power of focusing on creating something that is unique to each student. The activities ignite, personalize, and focus learning on what's most important for the student, producing work that is connected but pushing the student to achieve more.

Thanks to Judi for pulling together ideas and activities, which encourage creative and collaborative learning. If you're looking to make students think, it's here. If you're hoping to make student work productively in a collaborative way, it's here. If you're looking to encourage "ah-ha moments' in each student's learning, it's here. In short, the inroads that help a student define his/her creative process and take thinking to the highest level start with the intellectual freedom found in the exercises and projects.

Judi may not be a famous chef but she has cooked-up a way to make your life easier. You'll have well selected ingredients, a well-developed process, and products that display the kind of creative thinking that validates student learning in multiple quantifiable ways. It's a recipe for success educators strive to achieve. Bon appetite!

by Carla Aguilar, PhD

Judi Hofmeister is a skilled performing-arts educator who demonstrates commitment to her students and education in all that she does. In her experience teaching vocal music, theatre, and dance, Judi has crafted her career to feature creativity. She lives in a creative space, seeking opportunities to use the creativity that is naturally part of her. She is a role model for those who want to include creativity and learner-centered teaching in their performing-arts classroom.

In this book, Judi outlines exercises, games, and strategies that will help any performing-arts educator or leader reconceptualize how to include creativity as a part of lessons in a series of cake recipes. Some of the activities are straightforward and will be used in one class period, allowing the cake baking to happen quickly; others will be used in a longer sequence of lessons, allowing students to think more carefully about the ingredients, flavors, and presentation of the final product. Judi outlines ways to think about these activities but guides the decision-making back to the educator or leader to assist the students in the creative process.

This is not a book that you will look at once and then put on your shelf; it will become one of your go-to resources to develop, conceptualize, and determine creative actions in your classroom or studio. Each time you look at the exercises, you will be able to implement them just as Judi describes—or better yet, you will be able use these activities as a starting point for cultivating some creative exercises of your own to implement.

In this book, Judi reminds us that each of us is creative and has the ability to include creativity as a regular part of our teaching. Creativity isn't just something we do; it is integral to the performance process and a necessary aspect of all of the performing arts. You are about to open a cabinet with unlimited cake-baking ingredients. I am sure what you put to use will be delicious.

Carla Aguilar, PhD, is the director of music education at Metropolitan State University of Denver and a devoted believer in the power of creativity in the performing-arts classroom.

ACKNOWLEDGMENTS

There are several people I want to thank—without them, I would not be who I am today. From family members to coworkers to my dear friends, they have shaped my world and allowed me to be me. They have encouraged me to grow, explore, and discover my love of the creative process in all the areas I've chosen to experience. The paths I've taken have been rich with fun and fulfilling discoveries in which my soul has been filled to the brim. I am eternally grateful for Ernest, Peggy, Brent, Gary, and Marie Hofmeister; Dixie and Butch Rud; Mark Nelson; Robert Johnson; Scott Winters; Lisa Lefebvre-Perez; Laurie Seigmund; Patrick Garcia; Holly Kennedy; Pat Gosch; Bill McHale; Dr. Denina Brown; Edna Doherty; Judy Westerberg; Deborah Wick; Dr. Carla Holland; Karie Johnston; Michael Vahle; Mitch Samu; Dr. Carla Aguilar; Dr. Donna Goodwin; and Karol Gates. You color my world beautiful and make it a better place to live!

INTRODUCTION

My name is Judi Hofmeister. I have always been a creative sort of person. Even while growing up in a small farming community, I was always singing and dancing around my house. So it was pretty natural that after graduating high school, I went to college and studied Musical Theatre. Two weeks after I graduated college, I was fortunate enough to jump right into a ten year professional performing arts career. However, one summer day while onstage during a very hot matinee performance, I decided to go back to college and get my certification to teach theatre in the public schools. It was time for me to give back for all the wonderful learning I had experienced during my school days.

For twenty years I taught various performing arts classes at a high school in Colorado. I had the honor and the pleasure of teaching four years of vocal music and twenty years of dance and theatre, with the final thirteen years spent developing and implementing an International Baccalaureate (IB) Dance Program. After I retired from the classroom I embarked upon a career working with teachers as the Dance/Drama and Theatre Arts Consultant for the Colorado Department of Education. For the past six years I have facilitated writing and implementing arts standards, curriculum, and assessments, as well as provide consultation, training and professional development in arts integration.

I have researched various perspectives and theories of the Creative Process and developed activities for my students and teachers in all the areas in which I've taught. In this book, I share my "recipes for imagination"—exercises I've either gathered from other artists and teachers or created and developed myself. All the exercises in this book have helped my students in finding unique and original characters, creative movement, music composition, or cultural and thematic performances. These exercises have also been used when facilitating professional development for teachers. They can be used with all levels of performing arts experience and multiple styles of learners.

The exercises are designed as "recipes" that you can use in any order at any time in your own classrooms, workshops or rehearsals. They not only align to state and national arts standards, these exercises embody Essential Life Skills (or 21 century skills) and the philosophies of Michelle and Robert Root-Bernstein in their book *Sparks of Genius: Thirteen Thinking Tools of Creative People*. The exercises will ignite your students' imaginations and get them engaged in the creative process while having a ton of fun.

In this second edition I added several new components, which include: Connecting the Creative Process to Educational Standards, High Impact Instructional Strategies for the classroom, Arts Integration ideas, and Assessment Rubrics. I dive into more educational theory and clarify the connections of the Creative Process to multiple areas of educational practice. It is my hope that teachers will be able to utilize this new edition as a type of workbook, for not only collaborating with teachers in other content areas, but to aid in planning well rounded lessons that benefit all types of learners. With the addition of the Every Student Succeeds Act (ESSA) in 2015, it is more important than ever to integrate the Creative Process and arts concepts into every content area for a well-rounded education.

So, as you will learn by my cake baking analogy, from the beginning of gathering ingredients, to how they are mixed together and baked, to how the final product is frosted and decorated, *Cake Baking and the Creative*

Process Too is a fun way to savor and digest every morsel of a flavorful, fun lesson plan and overall creative project with your students. Have a great time baking your own creative cakes!

CAKE BAKING: THE PROCESS

When I was teaching I was always thinking of ways to describe the Creative Process to my high school students. Whenever I tried to give a regular explanation to them, their attention waned and they truly could've cared less about learning any type of process for creativity. Early one morning I woke up and had an "aha" moment. Teenagers can relate to food...so I got busy developing an analogy of how the creative process is like baking a cake from scratch. Once introducing them to this analogy, they easily began to understand the correlation from baking a cake to the artistic process:

1. First, decide what flavor of cake to make (the idea/inspiration for the project).
2. Second, gather the ingredients (the research, scripts, music, etc.).
3. Next, as a group, go about mixing these ingredients (developing blocking, choreography, lyrics, and music).
4. After all ingredients are mixed, put the creation in the oven to bake (rehearsals—refining and perfecting a scene, dance, or song).
5. Once the cake is baked and has had time to cool, apply the icing (costumes, sets, makeup).
6. Your cake, or project, is now ready to be consumed (performance).
7. DIGESTION (reflecting and evaluating the process).
8. Clean the kitchen (generating new ideas for the next project).

I have always told my students that the final two steps in this process are some of the most important parts of the entire creation. These are the steps that often inadvertently get left out or ignored all together: digestion and cleaning the kitchen. It is *very* important to have downtime after completing a performance to digest, reflect on, and evaluate the success of the final product. This is such an important step to not only completing the creative process but also allowing time to fill yourself back up with ideas and inspiration for the next project. This downtime allows for evaluation of the finished work as well as generating new creative ideas. Many times, the young artist wants to rush headlong into baking the next "cake." Taking time to put closure on one project before the next one has begun is integral to a successful end product.

CONNECTING CREATIVE PROCESS TO EDUCATIONAL STANDARDS

The Creative Process easily connects to educational standards and concepts, so no matter what you teach, if you stay true to the process, you really can't go wrong. I have found multiple connections with my cake baking analogy and the National Core Arts Standards (NCAS), Bloom's Taxonomy, various state's arts standards, and even linking it to Scientific Method. In the work that I do for my state's education department, I have the opportunity to not only work with arts educators, but general education teachers, as well as district leaders and school administrators. I have found my analogy of the process has also helped when evaluating teachers in the classroom, and for bridging gaps when differentiating multiple levels of student learners, such as students who are identified as Gifted and Talented. The analogy is easy to understand yet, encompasses many Essential Life Skills and arts concepts. This section will highlight many of the connections the Creative Process has to academic learning.

THE NATIONAL CORE ARTS STANDARDS (NCAS)

The National Core Arts Standards or NCAS were adopted in 2014 for any state, district, school, or educator. The NCAS were developed as a guide to unify quality academic standards in Dance, Drama, Media Arts, Music, and Visual Arts. In January of 2017, fifteen states had either adopted the NCAS, or have used the NCAS as one of their revision sources. It is easy to pick out multiple nuances of the Creative Process in all areas of the NCAS. Thank you to all who sat on the committee and developed a common, national arts resource for educators in our country!

NATIONAL CORE ARTS STANDARDS

Dance, Media Arts, Music, Theatre And Visual Arts

What Are The Standards?

A process that guides educators in providing a unified quality arts education for students in Pre-K through high school.

Read more →

Creating

Cr

■ Anchor Standard #1. Generate and conceptualize artistic ideas and work.

■ Anchor Standard #2. Organize and develop artistic ideas and work.

■ Anchor Standard #3. Refine and complete artistic work.

Performing/ Presenting/ Producing

Pr

■ Anchor Standard #4. Analyze, interpret, and select artistic work for presentation.

■ Anchor Standard #5. Develop and refine artistic work for presentation.

■ Anchor Standard #6. Convey meaning through the presentation of artistic work.

Responding

Re

■ Anchor Standard #7. Perceive and analyze artistic work.

■ Anchor Standard #8. Interpret intent and meaning in artistic work.

■ Anchor Standard #9. Apply criteria to evaluate artistic work.

Connecting

Cn

■ Anchor Standard #10. Synthesize and relate knowledge and personal experiences to make art.

■ Anchor Standard #11. Relate artistic ideas and works with societal, cultural and historical context to deepen understanding.

SCIENTIFIC METHOD VS CREATIVE PROCESS

- Ask a question (find the inspiration)
- Research the topic (gather the ingredients)
- Form a hypothesis(mix the ingredients)
- Test your hypothesis (experiment, play)
- Observe your data and draw a conclusion (rehearse and refine)
- Share or report your findings (perform)

BLOOM'S TAXONOMY OF LEARNING

In 1956 Benjamin Bloom devised a classification system of the skills used when actively learning. At the time Bloom had developed the six levels as: Knowledge, Comprehension, Application, Analysis, Synthesis and Evaluation. He placed these six skills into a pyramid and called it Bloom's Taxonomy. This was the system educators used to create lesson plans for decades. As you might notice, there is no mention of creativity in the 1956 version of Bloom's Taxonomy. It wasn't until the 1990's that Bloom's classification system was revised, the nouns were replaced with verbs, and the six levels were renamed: Remembering, Understanding, Applying, Analyzing, Evaluating, and Creating was placed on the top of the pyramid.

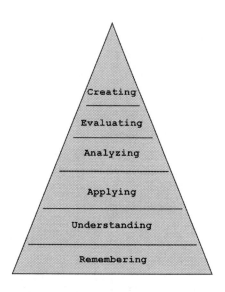

I remember a day when I was teaching, during a professional development workshop on the revised Bloom's Taxonomy. I got very excited that Creating had been placed at the top of the pyramid. It felt that what arts educators had always been doing in the classroom was finally being recognized as beneficial. Up to that point it felt as if arts education had been looked at as only "fun" and wasn't "important" or "real" learning. Now, with Bloom's revision, it was apparent that there was value to being creative and it was the highest level of thinking that we do as humans! I was elated!

At the same time as the introduction of Bloom's revision I was also in the midst of traveling to Cardiff, Wales to sit on the First Phase of the Dance Subject Committee for the newly developed International Baccalaureate (IB) Dance curriculum. To this day, that one experience has shaped my future educational career more than any other experience. I was one of eleven educators that were on the ground level of planning, writing and piloting a global IB dance curriculum that is now taught world-wide. What an amazing time in my life! What synchronicity that Bloom's revision had just debuted and I was embarking on one of the most creative times in my career! The concept of the Creative Process had just knocked on my door and I welcomed it in like an old friend.

SPARKS OF GENIUS

While Bloom's Taxonomy was being revised, two professors at Michigan State University, Michelle and Robert Root-Bernstein, were in the process of researching creativity and writing a book called *Sparks of Genius: The Thirteen Thinking Tools of the World's Most Creative People*. This book outlines the great, creative musicians, scientists, architects, and such, as embodying thirteen "thinking tools" that shaped their processes of learning, inventing, composing, etc. The thirteen tools are:

- Observing
- Imagining
- Abstracting
- Recognizing Patterns
- Forming Patterns
- Analogizing
- Body Thinking
- Empathizing
- Dimensional Thinking
- Modeling
- Playing
- Transforming
- Synthesizing

These thirteen traits transfer so easily to arts standards, the Creative Process, and to any arts integrated project! As I stated above, staying true to the process, incorporating these traits, linking them to Bloom's and any arts standards will have you and your students not only thinking like artists, but also sparking your own genius traits in no time!

THE IMPORTANCE OF PLAY IN THE ARTS CLASSROOM

If you want creative workers, give them enough time to play. –John Cleese

I don't know about you, but when I was a kid I loved to play. My father owned 3,800 acres of land that he farmed and ranched. From a young age I accompanied him to the farm almost on a daily basis. In the summer he would let me play in the creek, on the tractors as he plowed the fields, then sled down snowy hills in the winter. He taught me how to ride horses, and when I was older he gave me a small motorcycle that I learned to drive all around our farm. I would even help him heard cattle on that motorcycle. I loved playing at our farm, but one of my favorite things to do was to pretend I was a ballerina or Gene Kelly while splashing around in puddles, singing and dancing in the rain. There were no youth theatre groups or dance studios in my small hometown, so I had to be creative. I had quite an imagination and loved to use what I had around me to make-believe. My house and our farm were the perfect spots for me to play and be as creative as I wanted to be.

Now that I'm older and have not only professionally

performed onstage, but directed and taught performing arts, I find myself forgetting to play. As a teacher, I forget the importance of allowing my students to play as well. I have to remember just how important the concept of PLAY is when piecing together creative projects such as the school musical, a choir concert, a dance concert, or even a professional work day with teachers. It is integral to the student's self-discovery that they play throughout the process of creating and developing the multiple aspects of their performances and projects.

In 2000, the Creative Process and the concept of PLAY really hit home once I began working with my IB dance students as the pilot phase was first implemented. Since this was a brand new curriculum, we had no other choice but to learn side by side each other. I was just as much of a student as my dance students were. We were pretty much on an even playing field. So we played! Together we explored the intricacies of the Creative Process, as well as experimented with choreographic forms and structures. Together we researched and discovered distant world dance traditions. Together we "felt our way through the dark" towards the first round of performances for assessments. That was an exhilarating year! I think mostly because there was no right or wrong way of doing any of it. We were simply experiencing it all together for the first time.

The one thing I will never forget was how important it was that my students and I played, learned and practiced the Creative Process together. I was not the end-all, be-all source of information for them. They were gathering just as much information as I was and we were all learning together! At the end of that first year a lightbulb went off in my head: "I must always maintain this concept in my program. The students and I must always explore, discover and play together." For the next thirteen years I made sure to incorporate a good balance of structure to my lessons, but also room for play, or creative improvisation; always allowing my students to take the leadership role in certain areas of the process. I learned how to structure the concept of PLAY into quick exercises where the students could focus on the creative aspects of the assignment, task, or project I was asking of them. That's when I had the "aha" moment of the cake baking analogy for explaining the Creative Process. It was all in the concept of "play" for how I could convey this information to them and make it easy, usable, and fun.

So imagine my elation when I began researching Michelle and Robert Root-Bernstein's *Sparks of Genius: Thirteen Thinking Tools of the World's Most Creative People*. Imagine my complete joy when I saw that they had devoted an entire chapter to the concept of "Playing". I dove into that particular chapter with such fervor. I wanted to soak in every word. I not only learned that Alexander Fleming, the inventor of Penicillin, was simply playing with "bacterial paintings" when he happened on one of the world's first antibiotics, I also learned how the Root-Bernstein's broke down the concept of PLAY into three categories:

- Practice Play – Enhance skills through practice
- Symbolic Play – Play-acting, make-believe
- Game Play – Playing with rule-making

Imagine my overwhelming joy when I realized that, as a youth, I'd done ALL of these types of play, either out on our farm, in my own home, or at school with my friends. To add that Piaget suggested that the concept of PLAY strengthens various mental skills...well, I was over the moon! I was so grateful I'd allowed my students to play in all senses of the word! None of us even realized we were tapping into Bloom's highest levels of thinking and learning. We were simply having fun, honing the craft of our artwork, learning about other cultures by how they dance, and discovering new perspectives and techniques of dance making. I never imagined that we were sparking our own genius qualities! At the time I never imagined that having fun and playing in the arts classroom was really deep and important learning! I am now completely sold on the importance of PLAY!

THE DEPTH OF KNOWLEDGE (DOK) WHEEL

Once I had wrapped my brain around the importance of play and all its levels and nuances, I was looking at the Depth of Knowledge (DOK) wheel during a professional development work day. I wanted to see where PLAY resided. I looked through each level, and never found the word play. It wasn't there at all. That's when I started looking at the definition of PLAY and realized that it truly encompasses many of the verbs in the DOK wheel. Another light went on in my head, "PLAY is Level five!" PLAY gathers and encompasses many of the concepts in each level of the DOK wheel. Please take a moment to look at the wheel I have included. See how many concepts you can find that fit into the concept of PLAY. Circle each word. Have fun, feel free to add a few of your own that are not included in the wheel, which level would they be? Write them down in the space I have indicated, in whichever level you think they fit. You might even come back later to add more. That's great! That means your DOK wheel is a living, breathing reminder of the different types and layers of PLAY! Not to mention how the concept of play encompasses all levels of Bloom's Taxonomy. As you plan your units and/

or lessons make sure you are including verbs from all levels of the DOK wheel. To build a well-rounded artist, students need to develop skills from all the levels. If you have your students think (or create), do (perform), write (analyze), and discuss (reflect) on any of their lessons or projects, you will have included most learning styles. Your students will be immersed in well-rounded and well-balanced instruction that will make use of their unique ways of learning.

LEVEL 5

PLAY!

Jot down all the words in the DOK wheel that coincide with the word PLAY. Make sure to indicate which level they are in the DOK wheel. The goal is to utilize a good balance of concepts from each level. Then add a few of your own words.

Level 1   Level 2   Level 3   Level 4

How do I utilize each DOK level in my lessons?

WHAT IS BACKWARDS BY DESIGN AND ARTISTIC VISION?

It is very natural to the Creative Process to devise or determine an overall artistic vision for any project, big or small. The artistic vision allows the director to get an idea, or vision, of the "big picture". This vision helps the director to stay focused as they work their way through breaking down the steps and tasks of putting the project back together again as they work through creating the end performance.

In arts education we currently call this concept Project-Based Learning (PBL), but it's also known as "Backwards by Design". In Stephen R. Covey's 1989 book *The Seven Habits of Highly Effective People,* he defines Backwards by Design as:

"To begin with the end in mind means to start with a clear understanding of your destination. It means to know where you're going so that you better understand where you are now, so that the steps you take are always in the right direction."

A good artist and arts educator will envision what is wanted for the end product and makes plans towards that. Below is a good plan to follow:

1) Start with a strong artistic vision, or overall inspiration
2) Unpack how you want to get to that vision with learning activities, and tasks, etc. (this is the Creative Process)
3) Continue to review the original vision as you progress to the end product

This keeps not only the director/teacher focused, but the

group in which they are leading has a strong sense of what is expected for the end product. This type of planning is highly successful and a very natural, intuitive way to integrate artistic concepts into the core content area classroom.

To illustrate an easy way to use Backwards by Design in developing arts focused unit and lesson plans, I am going to introduce what I call a "storyboard" for planning, or mapping out a unit of study. In film and media arts the use of storyboards is common for not only illustrating the overall artistic vision, but for breaking down each segment, or scene that will be filmed. The storyboard is a great visual tool for the entire production crew and the basis of their process for creating any films, commercials, TV shows, etc.

I am developing this storyboard to coincide with my cake baking analogy so you can clearly see how the artistic vision fits into the Creative Process. Please look at the illustration below. It begins with the top left box, which is the overall artistic vision of the unit, or the end product...or as we say in education, the "performance assessment". Each box after the main vision is a "learning experience", a task/activity, or lesson that the students are assigned. Each box coincides with one of the steps I outlined earlier in my cake baking analogy: gather the ingredients, mix the ingredients, etc. After following the arrows and progressing through the learning experiences with your students, you are led right back to the initial artistic vision, which is the end product or the performance assessment. This shows that a true Creative Process is not linear in nature, it's circular and one "cycle's through" the process to get to the final performance. The final two boxes are after the performance assessment has taken place. That is the down time that I referred to earlier for digestion and cleaning the kitchen. This time is important to evaluate the success of the performances, to reflect on the process, and generate new ideas for the next project. All while digesting your "cake" and cleaning up after the project.

Overall idea/inspiration or artistic vision (Performance Assessment)

2) Gather Ingredients (Learning Experience 1)

3) Mix Ingredients (Learning Experience 2)

4) Put in the oven (Learning Experience 3) This step is the rehearsal process and may take more than 1 learning experience to complete. Feel free to add more learning experiences.

5) Apply the icing (Learning Experience 4)

6) Eat your cake! (Learning Experience 5) This is the Performance Assessment above

7) Digestion (Learning Experience 6) This is down time after the performance for evaluating

8) Clean the kitchen (Learning Experience 7) Time to generate new ideas

Unit Planning
Storyboard
Using
Backwards by Design

HIGH IMPACT INSTRUCTIONAL ARTS STRATEGIES

Up to now, I've been discussing a lot about the Creative Process and how it aligns with standards, other concepts and theories, how to work through the process, as well as how to plan units using the process. Now I want to shift the perspective and discuss how to teach using Creative Process. I want to introduce a tool that my colleagues and I developed for our state education department. It has been a great visual aid for teachers to not only see which instructional strategies align with arts concepts, but also the skills in which the students develop when we teach using these high quality strategies.

On the first chart below the High Impact Instructional Arts Stragies are listed along the left side of the chart. I have found when working with teachers from any content area, but especially when discussing arts integration, most teachers are already using these strategies in their classrooms. However, they aren't aware that these strategies, such as *Cooperative Learning*, *Project-Based Learning*, and *Reflective Discussion* go hand in hand with artistic concepts.

Along the top of the chart are the Artistic Learning Skills that students develop when the instructional strategies are utilized. In the middle of the chart are a series of X's. Each X meets up with a strategy and a skill. This shows the direct link of how when a teacher uses these strategies during a lesson, the student is developing a particular skill in response to that strategy. I encourage you to circle which strategies you are already using in your classroom, then follow the X to see which skills your students are developing from your instruction.

The chart also works the other way around. If you start with which skills you'd like your students develop, then follow the X to see which teaching strategies will work the best to hone that skill, then you can implement that strategy into your lesson. This list of strategies and skills is infinite, you can add as many as you like. We just compiled this particular list as a tool for teachers to see how common strategies connect to developing artistic skill.

Artistic Learning Skills

Improvisation	Role Play	Conceptual and Project Based Learning	Encourage and Allow Exploration and Discovery	Inquiry-Based Questioning	Project-Based Questioning	Demonstration/ Modeling	Direct Instruction ("mini lesson")	Cooperative Learning	Concept Adaptation	Compare & Contrast	Investigation/Inquiry	Imagining/Artistic Vision/Brainstorming	Artistic Learning Skills
X	X		X	X	X			X	X			X	Imagining/ Develop Artistic Vision
X	X	X	X		X	X	X				X	X	Read, write & use vocabulary through disciplinary lens
X	X		X		X	X	X		X	X	X	X	Develop, ask, & answer disciplinary questions
X	X	X	X	X		X		X				X	Communicate/ Collaborate
			X	X	X			X		X	X	X	Gather & evaluate sources
			X	X	X			X		X	X	X	Analyze primary and secondary sources
			X	X		X	X	X				X	Organize information
X	X	X	X				X	X	X	X	X		Apply disciplinary techniques & concepts
X	X	X	X	X	X	X		X	X	X	X	X	Critical Thinking/ Decision Making
X	X	X	X	X	X	X	X	X	X	X	X	X	Developing/ Composing
			X	X	X			X		X		X	Identify multiple perspectives
		X	X	X	X			X	X	X	X	X	Refinement/ Creative Problem Solving
		X	X	X	X	X	X	X	X			X	Develop and refine work for presentation or display
		X	X	X	X	X	X	X		X	X		Develop performance/ display etiquette
		X	X	X	X			X		X	X		Self/Peer Assessment
		X	X	X	X	X	X	X		X	X		Evaluate process
		X	X	X	X			X		X	X	X	Reflect on finished product
		X	X	X	X	X			X	X			Self-Adjust

In the past I have had teachers ask what the definitions are for each strategy that is listed on this chart. So let me include some quick definitions here:

Imagining, Artistic Vision, Brainstorming – A very important aspect of the Creative Process! It is essential to begin every creative project using our imaginations to invision what the big picture is going to look like.

Investigation/Inquiry – This is the step after imagining or invisioning the big picture, where one begins to gather, investigate or inquire about what kinds of information needs to be included in the project. It is research.

Compare and Contrast – This is a great strategy for students to see the differences in everything from types of research, to the different types of art forms to use in their project. This strategy also helps in making comparisons to real world applications.

Concept Adaptation – In this strategy the teacher is asked to guide the students in adapting different perspectives to a single concept. It is used when looking at the project, or piece of art with different lenses.

Cooperative Learning – The arts are famous for cooperative learning! This is where students learn how to collaborate and work together. It is one of the most important life skills we need to learn!

Direct Instruction – This strategy is your basic lecture format. It is the teacher giving instruction or information to the student. An educator wants to be careful not to lean on this strategy for every lesson. While Direct Instruction has it's place in education, please make sure to differentiate your instruction and add other strategies to your lessons. A note for dance teachers: Direct Instruction is what we do when we demonstrate movement in a dance technique class. That is the dance teachers version of Direct Instruction.

Demonstration/Modeling – This strategy is also used

frequently in the dance classroom. This strategy is integral to arts instruction! It is very important that young artists see demonstrations of not only what is being created, but how the artist uses their creative process to get to the end product. This strategy helps to inspire the young artist and model how their creative process can be developed.

Project Based Questioning – This strategy is used to help the teacher keep an overall focus on the project by guiding the students to develop the "driving question". A driving question helps to communicate the overall purpose of the project in one very focused statement or question. This is commonly used when developing thesis statements, but is also used in the arts when pinpointing the overall focus of a creative project.

Inquiry Based Questioning – This strategy is used to help the teacher guide students to develop a series of questions for their research that evolve as the process of developing the project moves forward. These questions keep the student artist on track and organized as they delve into their artistic research.

Encourage and Allow Exploration and Discovery – This is pretty straightforward. Please allow students time to explore and discover. The arts are all about experimenting with different skills and ways of art making. I call this "play time". Allow your students time to find their artistic "voice", or develop their own process.

Conceptual and Project Based Learning – This is a strategy that I discussed more in-depth in the Backwards by Design section. It is linked to developing an artistic vision and ways of working towards the big picture.

Role Play – Again, this strategy is pretty straight forward, especially in the performing arts. Allow time for students to physically role play. This is utilized a lot in theatrical practices for developing character, etc. Students may also benefit from role playing historical aspects of the research they are doing for a particular project. Role playing allows them to think with their whole body, or as the Root-Bernsteins call it, "Body Thinking".

Improvistaion – Another way to role play, allowing students to improvise their way through situations. There are many improvisational theatre games that can be adapted for teaching in the core academic content areas. I have included several improv games in this book in the Theatre Cake section. Dancers and musicians also utilize improvisation when choreographing and composing.

Evaluative/Organized Critiques – This strategy is important for analyzing not only the Creative Process of developing any project or lesson, but also for evaluating the success of a performance, or finished artistic product. Giving time for feedback is essential in the Creative Process.

Reflective Discussion – I used this strategy almost every day in my dance, theatre and vocal music classes and rehearsals. I also used this at the end of every large project. A time for reflection is also an essential part of the Creative Process.

Establish and Link Background Knowledge – The Creative Process is not a linear progression through a list of tasks that need to be completed in a project. The Creative Process is a cycle that encompasses and utilizes knowledge and skills that have been developed from other creative projects. This strategy asks the teacher to guide the students to establishing connections and links to what they already know. This allows students to discover how their art connects to the real world.

Create Real-World and Personal Relevance – Where else in our lives does the Creative Process apply? Everywhere! This strategy asks the teacher to guide the student artist in revealing ways that they can use their artistic skills in every day life. In what other ways can they collaborate? What other ways can they creatively solve a problem. The Creative Process can be applied everywhere, every day!

In this next chart I took the information from the High Impact Instructional Strategy chart and put it side by side with my cake baking analogy of the Creative Process. So now you not only see where in the proecss it is good to use certain High Impact Instructional Strategies, but also the skills students are developing as they progress through the process as its being taught using quality strategies. If you have not taught an arts focused project, this is a great map for knowing how to teach during the Creative Process.

Putting It All Together

CREATIVE PROCESS (How we create)	INSTRUCTIONAL STRATEGIES (How you teach)	SKILLS (What students know & do)
1) Decide flavor (inspiration)	Imagining, brainstorming, develop artistic vision, Direct Instruction	Imagine, develop artistic vision, inquiry, decision making, communicate/collaborate
2) Gather ingredients (research)	Investigation, Inquiry, Direct Instruction, Project Based Questioning, Inquiry Based Questioning	Read, write, use vocabulary, inquiry, communicate/collaborate, gather resources, organize information.
3) Mix ingredients (develop structure)	Compare/Contrast, Concept Adaptation, Cooperative Learning, Encourage & Allow Exploration/Discovery, Improvisation	Apply techniques & concepts, communicate/collaborate, creative problem solving/critical thinking.
4) Bake the cake (rehearsal process)	Demonstration/Modeling, Cooperative Learning, Encourage & Allow Exploration/Discovery	Apply techniques & concepts, communicate/collaborate, creative problem solving/critical thinking, refine work for performance
5) Cool/apply icing (costumes, make-up)	Cooperative Learning, Encourage & Allow Exploration/Discovery	Identify multiple perspectives, develop/refine work for performance, develop performance etiquette
6) Consume (performance)	Role Play, Create Real World & Personal Relevance	Develop performance etiquette/skills, self/peer assessment, evaluate process
7) Digest (reflect, evaluate)	Evaluative Critiques, Reflective Discussion, Establish & Link Background Relevance	Self/peer assessment, evaluate process, reflect on finished product, self-adjust

Above is a snapshot of how the Creative Process can drive High Impact Instructional Strategies.

Also included are the skills that the Creative Process and Instructional Strategies could draw from students.

A final note concerning instructional strategies: I think it is important to remember what you are already doing in your instruction for your students and see how that aligns with artistic concepts. It is daunting and overwhelming to try and "clear the slate" and feel as if you need to start over just to incorporate thinking and teaching like an artist. That's unnecessary, overwhelming and, frankly, not needed. Look at the good things you are already bringing to your classroom on a daily basis, incorporate a couple of new strategies with each new project, follow the Creative Process as best as you can, and remember to play! You will soon be layering, or scaffolding, your lessons with quality, arts focused concepts, learning experiences, and strategies. Soon you'll be baking your own creative cake! I am including a quick lesson planning guide to help you not only plan your lessons, but to include which instructional strategies go in which part of the lesson, as well as pinpointing where in the Creative Process you are, and which skills the students will be developing during their learning.

Creative Process	Lesson Plan Guide
Which steps of the creative process align with the objective?	Objective / Learning Experience: (Key knowledge & skills students will master in the lesson) • A quick summary of the focus of the lesson
Which steps in the creative process align with the Instructional strategies used in this lesson?	Instructional Strategy List: (Choose from the Instructional Strategies chart.) • List discipline-specific strategies used for this lesson • List the skills students will develop during this lesson

This is completed in the first 3-7 minutes of the lesson. The introduction should align with explaining the artistic vision of the overall project.	Opening Introduction: (How will you introduce the lesson?) Instructional Strategy chosen:
Which steps of the creative process align with the body of the lesson?	Body of the lesson: (list details of the activity or learning experience.) Instructional Strategies chosen: Skills students will develop:
The closing activity reinforces learning. This should align with step 7 in the Creative Process.	Closure: (How will students reflect on their learning?) Instructional Strategy chosen:
Formative assessment will be a quick Check for Understanding in which students will demonstrate they are on track.	Formative Assessment: Formative Assessment tool/method: Learning indicators of success: (What evidence is there that shows the student is approaching the learning target?)

Okay, now it's playtime! The next four sections of this book focus on exercises and ideas that I either developed myself, or gathered from other teachers or artists. These exercises and projects truly are the "tried and true" activities that worked time and again with many different levels of students, as well as for professional development workshops with teachers. I designed these sections as a quick go-to for teachers, substitute teachers, or anyone who leads rehearsals and creative workshops. The exercises and projects build group cohesion, as well as develop multiple Essential Life Skills and they directly align with not only the Creative Process, but arts standards. Have fun! Now go PLAY!

The Dance Cake

God creates, I do not create. I assemble and I
steal everywhere to do it—from what I see, from
what the dancers can do, from what others do.
—George Balanchine

IN THIS SECTION

If I were to put a label on my IB dance program as a description of what we did, I would have to say that it comes closest to what has been referred to as "dance theatre." My dance curriculum was a unique blend of creative movement exercises, technique classes, choreographic development and analysis, research of contemporary dance styles, and world dance traditions. The curriculum is also well immersed in performance and production skills. It sounds like a lot, and it is, but my IB dance curriculum was a two-year program, so there was more time for exploration and discovery.

Here are some fun exercises that help the student dancer begin thinking creatively. Please use these exercises in any way that fits into your own program. Remember, this is about your creative process, which is unique! Please scribble, sketch, doodle, and take notes in this book. Use it as your creative journal as you progress with your students through these exercises. Also, please feel free to adapt and abstract these exercises however you may wish. It's all about thinking creatively and about dancing on the "other side of the barre." Enjoy!

The Name Dance
Level: Beginner

Ingredients
3–5 dancers

Instructions
   The dancers select the name of one person in their group. They must work together to create the shapes of each letter in the chosen name. The dancers need to use multiple levels and different directions and develop moving transitions between each letter. The group also needs to create a beginning, middle, and ending to this dance. You may add music or not. (Creates a 1- to 2-minute dance)

Skills Used in This Exercise
- problem-solving creatively with a group
- making decisions
- using movement to symbolize a letter
- applying knowledge of basic choreographic structure (beginning, middle, ending)
- effectively using space, time, and energy
- understanding the concept of transition
- exploring movement in different directions and levels

NOTES

Shape, Shape, and Reshape
Level: Beginner to Intermediate

Ingredients
> 3–5 dancers
> Three different shapes (e.g., spiral, triangle, arrow)

Instructions

The dancers in each group need to create movement to symbolize the shapes selected by the instructor. They must work together to create the first shape, transition into the second shape, and finish smoothly with the third. They need to use multiple levels, different directions, and floor patterns, as well as develop moving transitions from one shape to the next. In other words, the group needs to become a human lava lamp. Make sure the group creates a beginning, middle, and ending to this dance. You may add music to this dance or not. (Creates a 1- to 2-minute dance)

Skills Used in This Exercise
- problem-solving creatively with a group
- making decisions
- using movement to symbolize a shape
- applying knowledge of basic choreographic structure (beginning, middle, ending)
- effectively using space, time, and energy
- understanding the concept of transition
- exploring movement in different directions, levels, and floor patterns

NOTES

Emotions Dance
Level: Intermediate to Advanced

Ingredients
2–6 dancers

Select emotions (e.g., surprise, anxiety, longing) and select music to go with each emotion (instrumental music is best, 2–3 minutes).

Instructions
The dancers in each group are given an emotion and music selected by the instructor. They must work together to create the movement that symbolizes the selected emotion. The dancers need to explore gestures used with that emotion and adapt those gestures into movement, using multiple levels and different directions. The group also needs to create a beginning, middle, and ending to this dance.

Skills Used in This Exercise
- problem-solving creatively with a group
- making decisions
- incorporating gestures to movement to symbolize an emotion
- applying knowledge of basic choreographic structure (beginning, middle, ending)
- effectively using space, time, and energy
- exploring movement with different gestures, directions, and levels

NOTES

Elements of Nature
Level: Beginner to Advanced

Ingredients

    1–6 dancers (a more advanced level to this exercise is to
      have each dancer perform solo)

    Instrumental music that complements the chosen
      element of nature (approximately 3–4 minutes)

Instructions

    The dancers choose an element of nature to portray in this piece (either as a group or individually). Participants must work to create movement that symbolizes the element of nature. The dancers need to develop movement with multiple levels, rhythms, different directions, and floor patterns. Each piece also needs a beginning, middle, and ending.

Skills Used in This Exercise

- problem-solving creatively
- making decisions
- using movement to symbolize an element of nature
- applying knowledge of basic choreographic structure (beginning, middle, ending)
- effectively using space, time, and energy
- understanding the concept of intent and motif
- exploring movement with different rhythms, textures, and directions

NOTES

Random Dance
Level: Intermediate to Advanced

Ingredients
> 6–16 dancers (also works great with a dance class of 24)
> Foam graphing cubes for use as blank dice
> Multiple random, ambient electronic music pieces (2–3 minutes in length)

Instructions

Have the dancers pair up in partners and number the partnered groups 1 through 6. Give time for each group to do research on Merce Cunningham and the Chance Dance choreographic structure. Each group of partners will then develop three eight-counts of a movement phrase. Once the movement phrases are complete, put three to four of the partnered groups together to create a new, larger group of six to eight dancers. Give each of the larger groups a cube/dice with the numbers 1 through 6. Each group then rolls the dice to determine the order of the three eight-count phrases in the dance. Allow each group time to put the phrases together in any way they wish. Groups can learn each other's phrases if they want. Allow the dancers to experiment with this and decide how they wish to create their piece. Once the phrases have been put together, play a random piece of music as each group performs its piece. It's very fun to see what meaning comes from these random dance pieces.

Skills Used in This Exercise
- problem-solving creatively
- making decisions
- using random movement to create a dance piece
- understanding the concept of "layering" choreography
- exploring Merce Cunningham's Chance Dance choreographic structure

NOTES

Laban's Eight Theories of Effort
Level: Advanced

Ingredients
  1 dancer
  Laban's Eight Efforts, as follows: dab, flick, punch, slash, glide, float, wring, press
  Instrumental music, 2–3 minutes in length

Instructions

  This is a solo piece choreographed by a student dancer who will perform his or her own choreography. The dancer begins by doing in-depth, written research about Rudolph Laban, including historical information about his contribution to dance and his development of Labanotation. The dancer then creates the movement for a two- to three-minute solo using Laban's Eight Efforts throughout the piece.

Skills Used in This Exercise
  • problem-solving creatively using specific movements
  • applying knowledge of basic choreographic structure (beginning, middle, ending)
  • effectively using space, time, and energy
  • understanding the concept of transition
  • exploring the concept of different dynamics of movement
  • exploring movements in different directions and levels

NOTES

Questions for Discussion

(Questions can also be used as a written evaluation.)

1. What were you trying to express in your piece? Why?

2. How did you get the idea or inspiration?

3. What was your biggest challenge? Why?

4. Describe how you problem-solved any issues you might have had.

5. What part of the process was the most interesting? Why?

6. How did you contribute to the collaboration?

7. What level are you as a dancer?

8. What have you learned about yourself in this exercise?

9. Were you satisfied with your performance? Why or why not?

10. Discuss any changes you would make to your work and why you would make them.

43

The Theatre Cake

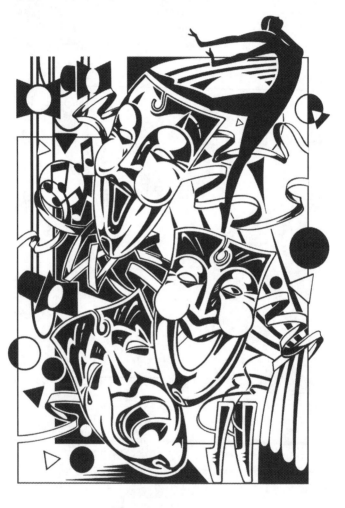

I believe in imagination.
—Meryl Streep

IN THIS SECTION

The performing-arts department of which I'd been a part for twenty years is a popular program at our school. We not only produced six to eight shows a year, but we also hosted a one-act festival, a battle-of-the-bands contest, and a comedy improvisation competition—or what is known in our neck of the woods as "Comedy Sports." All of the theatre exercises in this section are taken from our improv show. We begin teaching a few of these exercises very early in our Theatre I class and add more games that follow through until our Theatre III class. This is when the student actors create multiple improv groups, and the games are played as a sport or competition between groups.

While these exercises (or games) work well on their own, one can also put these together to create an entire improv comedy unit that can last three to four weeks. Again, please be creative in the way you use these exercises. Create your own comedy-sports evening of fun. It's a great fund-raiser! The student actors *love* playing these games, and the audience laughs the evening away.

Let the competition begin!

Stop, Freeze!
Level: Beginner to Advanced

Ingredients
  5–7 actors

Instructions

One of the actors is designated as the referee and is given the task of saying "stop, freeze," as well as getting a suggestion of a situation from the audience. Two actors at a time begin to play out the scenario until the referee says, "stop, freeze", and stops them. The actors must freeze in their final pose of that scene while a new actor takes the place of one of the actors and starts a different scene. The group rotates through each actor two or three times.

This is a good warm-up game.

Skills Used in This Exercise
  - problem-solving creatively with a partner
  - making quick decisions
  - listening to your partner and the referee
  - vocal projection
  - creating multiple characters
  - creating multiple situations/scenarios
  - pantomiming or showing physical animation

NOTES

What Are You Doing?
Level: Beginner to Advanced

Ingredients
4–6 actors

Instructions

Two actors at a time take turns asking each other, "What are you doing?" One actor replies that he or she is doing a task, such as "brushing my teeth." The other actor needs to pantomime that task and then ask the other actor, "What are you doing?" That actor then pantomimes the task that was said. Each actor goes back and forth in this manner until one of them hesitates. The actor who hesitates sits down and is replaced by a new actor who asks, "What are you doing?" And then a new round is played. This game can go on until all actors have had a chance to participate.

This is a good warm-up game.

Skills Used in This Exercise
- problem-solving creatively with a partner
- making quick decisions
- listening to your partner
- vocal projection
- pantomiming simple tasks

NOTES

Forward/Reverse
Level: Intermediate to Advanced

Ingredients
    3–5 actors

Instructions

    One of the actors is designated as the referee and is given the task of saying "forward" or "reverse," as well as getting a suggestion of a situation for a scene from the audience. Two to four actors then begin to play out the scenario until the ref calls out, "Reverse." The actors must reverse the order of the scene. The referee then calls out, "Forward," and the actors must play the action of the scene going forward, starting at the point where the referee called out. This continues in this fashion as the referee randomly calls out, "Forward" and "Reverse," until the referee ends the scene. (When working with more advanced actors, the referee can also include the directions of "fast-forward" or "slow-mo reverse." This makes the scene very funny to watch!)

Skills Used in This Exercise
- problem-solving creatively with a group
- making quick decisions
- listening to your group and the referee
- vocal projection
- creating characters
- memorizing a scene quickly

NOTES

Sportscaster
Level: Intermediate to Advanced

Ingredients
   5–7 actors

Instructions

   Two of the actors are designated as the sportscasters. They will offer play-by-play commentary during the game. They are also given the task of getting a suggestion of a household task (such as lawn-mowing) from the audience. The sportscasters then begin their commentary for the "First Annual Olympic Games of Lawn-Mowing". The three to five additional actors begin to play out the scene as the lawn-mowing "athletes," silently pantomiming the movement. They begin with "warm-ups", proceed to pantomiming the "race," and then at the finish line, their competitive natures overtake them and they proceed to battle with the winner of the race—all in slow motion! All the athletes' movements are performed in slow motion. The sportscasters are the decision-makers of when to end the game by "going to a commercial break," as the athletes tackle the winner at the finish line in slow motion.

Skills Used in This Exercise
   * problem-solving creatively with a group
   * making quick decisions
   * listening to the sportscasters
   * pantomiming in slow motion
   * showing physical and facial animation

NOTES

Hitchhiker
Level: Beginner to Advanced

Ingredients
   5–7 actors

Instructions

One of the actors is designated as the driver and is given the task of getting a suggestion of five to seven emotions from the audience, as well as getting a suggestion of a mode of transportation, such as a canoe. Each actor is assigned an emotion, and the actor who is the driver begins the scene as driver of the canoe. One at a time, the actors begin to "hitchhike" to get into the canoe. As each actor enters the canoe, all the actors in the canoe must take on that actor's assigned emotion. The group plays out this scene until everyone is "in the boat." Then, one by one, each actor leaves, and the group left in the canoe must take on the emotions in reverse order until the only person left is the driver.

Skills Used in This Exercise
   • problem-solving creatively with a group
   • making quick decisions
   • listening to your group
   • creating characters based on an emotion
   • creating a theme based on an emotion
   • showing physical animation in a confined space

NOTES

Slide Show
Level: Beginner to Advanced

Ingredients
   5–7 actors

Instructions

   One of the actors is designated as the referee and is given the task of getting a suggestion of a vacation spot (such as the pyramids) from the audience. The referee is also in charge of running the "remote" for the "slide show." The remaining actors begin to work together to make the images of the pictures from the vacation until the referee says "click" and changes to the next slide. The actors must freeze in a pose for each picture until the next slide is "clicked." The referee decides when the slide show is over and the game is done.

Skills Used in This Exercise
   •   problem-solving creatively with a group
   •   making quick decisions of shapes and images
   •   listening to the referee
   •   creating multiple scenarios in tableau
   •   showing physical and facial animation

NOTES

Spelling Bee
Level: Beginner to Advanced

Ingredients
    5–6 actors
    4–5 chairs, or a place for 4–5 actors to sit

Instructions
One of the actors is designated as the referee and is given the task of getting a suggestion of an interesting word from the audience (such as supercalifragilisticexpialidocious). Three to five actors at a time sit next to each other and, from stage right to stage left, begin to spell the word one letter at a time. Once the group is finished spelling the word, they say the word together. This lets the referee know that they are finished spelling the word, and the referee can then ask for another word from the audience and the next round of spelling can occur. There should only be five to six rounds of this game before the referee thanks the audience for coming to this evening's spelling bee.

This is a great cool-down game.

Skills Used in This Exercise
- problem-solving creatively with a group
- making quick decisions
- listening to your group and the referee
- vocal projection
- working together to spell words one letter at a time

NOTES

Questions for Discussion
(Questions can also be used as a written evaluation.)

1. What was your favorite game to play? Why?

2. What gave you the ideas or inspiration to create a certain character or scene?

3. What was your biggest challenge? Why?

4. Describe how you problem-solved any problems you might have had.

5. What part of the improvisational process was the most interesting? Why?

6. How did you contribute to the collaboration?

7. At what level are you as an actor?

8. What have you learned about yourself during these games?

9. Were you satisfied with your performances? Why or why not?

10. Discuss any changes you'd make to your work. Why would you make these changes?

The Vocal Cake

I go by instinct ... I don't worry about experience.
—Barbra Streisand

IN THIS SECTION

In college, I was a music theatre major, so I completed coursework in theatre, dance, and vocal music. Then I performed professionally before I began my teaching career. I'm actually certified to teach Theatre K–12, but I have enough hours to teach in the areas of dance and voice as well. This has been a great tool in my bag of tricks and has kept me employed through several transitions in our district and in our performing-arts department. I'm grateful for this versatility, not only as an artist but as an arts educator. It's kept me "gigging" all these years.

While I haven't taught choir as long as I've taught theatre and dance, I have had the opportunity to develop composition exercises and thematic concerts that have turned into successful performances and fund-raisers. These concerts can take six to eight weeks in class for preparation. I will also include a list of song ideas for each concert at the end of this book.

I've directed three choirs: a large mixed ensemble, a midsized women's choir, and a small mixed-voice swing choir. Each level of choir has its own focus during each concert, but all three choirs participated in my composition exercises. I found the exercises to be a fun, hands-on way to learn and apply music-theory skills.

Singing Telegrams
Level: Beginner to Advanced

Ingredients
  Singers in groups of 6–8 (two per vocal part)
  Valentine candy or roses

Instructions
  Each group composes singing telegrams for Valentine's Day using inspiration from pop songs or commercial jingles. Each group must include simple harmonies in their tune. (Optional: Each group must notate their short song and write out the lyrics.) At my school, we sell these singing telegrams for four dollars each and include either candy or a rose. Each group travels to the classrooms of the telegram recipients and performs the tune in costume, with movement. This activity has been a big hit and a good fund-raiser.
  This unit takes two to four weeks.

Skills Used in This Exercise
  • problem-solving creatively with a group
  • understanding basic music theory
  • using simple vocal techniques and harmonies
  • composing short jingles
  • developing a group theme
  • deciding on costumes and simple movement
  • performing

NOTES

ABA/Triads
Level: Intermediate to Advanced

Ingredients
Singers in groups of 8 (two per vocal part)
Blank staff paper
A handout of major, minor, diminished, and augmented
    triads in any key
Keyboard

Instructions

Each group composes a simple song using the verse/chorus—or ABA—song structure. Each group must use the four triads in the composition of their song and include simple harmonies in their tune. Each group must notate their short song and write out the lyrics. (This exercise works best when a singer who knows how to read music and play piano is assigned to each group.) When finished writing their songs, each group performs their song for the class.

This unit takes three to four weeks.

Skills Used in This Exercise
- problem-solving creatively with a group
- understanding basic music theory
- using simple vocal techniques and harmonies
- composing
- performing

NOTES

Big Band/USO Radio Show
Level: Beginner to Advanced

Ingredients
> Music selections from the big-band era. Andrew Sisters, patriotic, George M. Cohan, or Manhattan Transfer work well.

Instructions

This is a themed choir concert. All the music in this concert fits within the theme and format of an old-time radio show. When I developed this show, I assigned my students to research 1930s and 1940s radio shows along with the USO shows during World War II. The students wrote the script to the radio show, and I auditioned the students who would be the emcees for the concert.

I had three choirs—a mixed concert choir, a women's choir, and a mixed swing choir—and there were multiple levels of arrangements chosen for each choir. For example, my swing choir was the highest-level choir, and their music was the more-advanced Manhattan Transfer style of vocal arrangements. I ended this concert with a mass choir arrangement of "You're a Grand Old Flag," where the choirs marched down the aisles of the theatre, through the audience, with flags. This show was a successful crowd-pleaser.

Skills Used in This Exercise
- understanding basic to advanced music theory
- using vocal techniques and harmonies
- researching and creating a themed script
- researching costumes of the big-band era
- choreographing simple movement
- performing

NOTES

Nifty '50s/'60s Dinner Theatre
Level: Beginner to Advanced

Ingredients
> Music from the 1950s and 1960s
> Assorted props and set pieces to look like a soda shop,
> complete with a jukebox
> A parent or school group to organize the dinner, or a local
> restaurant to cater the event

Instructions

This themed dinner-theatre concert was a fund-raiser for my choir program. It was a huge success because of a wonderful group of parents who took on the organization of the spaghetti dinner and ticket sales.

This project is a large undertaking and takes multiple meetings with the parents to assure that all details have been worked out and people or students are assigned to all tasks. My students helped to serve beverages before the show while the audience members served themselves buffet-style. A group of parents helped to bus the tables while the students got in their costumes, and then it was showtime.

I ended this concert with a mass choir version of "Up, Up and Away." The singers stood among the audience singing the song, with purple balloons that they batted back and forth with each other and the audience. Everyone had a great time playing with the balloons, and the audience even began to sing along with the students.

Skills Used in This Exercise
- understanding basic to advanced music theory
- using vocal techniques and harmonies
- researching costumes and movement of the era
- organizing
- performing

NOTES

Madrigal Dinner Theatre
Level: Beginner to Advanced

Ingredients

Madrigal music from the Renaissance and early Baroque eras

A parent or school group to organize the dinner, or a local restaurant to cater the event

3–4 long tables with chairs, tablecloths, and settings to look like a Renaissance king's castle

Props like a large family crest and a boar's head can also be added

Instructions

This themed dinner-theatre concert was a fund-raiser. It is great to do this event during the holiday season. For this event, a local restaurant catered and served the food. The dinner served was simple baked chicken, baked potatoes, assorted grilled vegetables, bread, and flaming pudding for dessert. Drinks included a nonalcoholic Wassail punch.

The singers enter singing in a procession and then sit at the main table (the king's table) and sing madrigals throughout the evening as the dinner is served. Carols, such as "The Boar's Head," "Wassail, Wassail," and "The Flaming Pudding," can all be incorporated into this royal evening of musical fun.

Skills Used in This Exercise

- understanding basic to advanced music theory
- using vocal techniques and harmonies
- researching costumes and movement of the era
- organizing
- performing

NOTES

Victorian Carolers
Level: Intermediate to Advanced

Ingredients
    10–15 Victorian carols
    Singers in groups of 8 (two singers per vocal part)
    Assorted Victorian-era costume pieces
    Caroling books (optional)
    1 pitch pipe per group

Instructions

Each group learns ten to fifteen Victorian carols a cappella. Once the groups are fairly comfortable with their vocal parts, have them rehearse by strolling around your auditorium, classroom, outside (weather permitting), and the halls of the school to get practice for strolling and singing at the same time.

I booked my strolling carolers in nursing homes, at community holiday festivals, at outdoor malls, at other schools, and then had them stroll to different classes in our own school. (Please make sure to get permission if you're going to another classroom. Some teachers would rather not have their classes disrupted during finals preparation.)

Skills Used in This Exercise
- understanding basic to advanced music theory
- using a cappella vocal techniques, harmonies, and blending
- researching costumes and traditions of the era
- organizing
- performing

NOTES

Questions for Discussion
(Questions can also be used as a written evaluation.)

1. How did you feel that your telegram or song turned out? Explain.

2. What gave you the ideas or inspiration to create your lyrics and music?

3. What was your biggest challenge?

4. Describe how you problem-solved any challenges you might have had.

5. What part of the process was the most interesting?

6. How did you contribute to the collaboration?

7. At what level are you as a musician?

8. What have you learned about yourself during these exercises or performances?

9. Were you satisfied with your performances? Why or why not?

10. Discuss any changes you'd make to your work. Why?

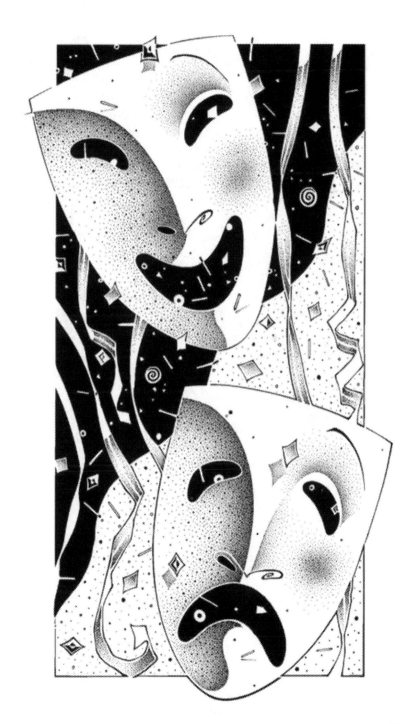

The Arts Integration Cake

Arts Integration allows us to build chefs who make
choices, not cooks who merely follow the recipe.
—Susan Riley

IN THIS SECTION

It is the supreme art of the teacher to awaken joy in creative expression and knowledge. --Einstein

For the past four years I've had the pleasure and honor to work as the Dance/Drama and Theatre Arts Consultant for the Colorado Department of Education (CDE). It has been a wonderful learning experience for me! I have had the opportunity to work not only with arts educators in multiple school districts in Colorado, but also teachers in neighboring states. When I first began this work, I was mainly focusing on professional development specifically for all grade levels of arts educators. However, through the years the focus has shifted and I have been working more and more with elementary teachers who wish to implement more arts into their everyday classroom instruction.

As I was putting together my first arts integration presentation, I wanted to begin with assuring the teachers that the arts are a "safe place", they should have nothing to fear, and just because they'd had little to no arts training, they could easily and quickly learn how to "think like artists". No matter what my focus is for any workshop, I always want to start with finding out what the teachers are currently doing in their instruction and build from that foundation. Having been a teacher for twenty years, I am all too familiar with how educators are always asked to do more, or add more to the load of what they are already doing. So I never want to overwhelm teachers. My goal is to give them new ideas and tools to put in their "bag of tricks" that will enhance what they are already doing. Hopefully these ideas will give them a breath of fresh air in their daily interaction with their students. It truly is one of my favorite things when I see the "aha" moments happening for teachers, and they get excited about new ways of thinking or doing things. I know their excitement will rub off on their students and everyone in their classroom will be excited about learning!

This section focuses on ideas to integrate arts into common core content areas. Having my IB background has really helped to develop units using Project-Based Learning and to plan lessons using the Backwards by Design concept. It has also helped me to look at an overall artistic project and find the connections or links to other content areas. So, to use a phrase my students have used, this section is "the big mash-up". Let's answer the question of how to creatively blend, or "mash-up" artistic concepts into common core content areas. Let's see what new recipes of imagination can be created!

CONTENT AREAS

Below is a table with the content areas that I feel are the easiest to integrate artistic practices and implement the Creative Process. As I said in the introduction to this section, this is the big "mash-up". There is no right or wrong way to blend or mash-up these content areas. Start with what interests you and go from there. In the true fashion of Backwards by Design, begin with selecting an overall theme or vision, then decide which perspective, or content areas, you'd like to explore. If this is the first time you've done anything like this, begin with what you know, then you can branch out into undiscovered territory in a different project. If this is the first chapter you are reading in this book, please make sure to go back to the section titled *Cake*

Baking: The Process and read through to the end of the *High Impact Instructional Strategies* section. This will help you to know how to plan a large creative project.

If you have done this before, start with a theme you've never taught. Step outside of the box and pull in a couple of concepts or ideas that are a bit foreign...literally! Go to the corners of our world and incorporate a theme from a different culture. Work through the Creative Process, and as I said earlier in this book, become a student with your students. Learn side by side each other. It is an awesome experience and your students will find things, or think of things you never would have. Doing an arts integrated project is also a great way to collaborate with other educators. So have fun, be creative, share the gathering of the information, and enjoy the journey!

Common Core	Arts
History	Dance
Language Arts	Drama
Math	Media Arts
Science	Music
(Which content areas do you want to blend?)	Visual Arts

IDEAS FOR THEMED, CULTURAL PROJECTS

First, let me give you a little background as to how I came up with the ideas I am sharing in this section. As I stated earlier, I taught IB dance, which is a pre-collegiate, world-wide dance curriculum that is taught during the junior and senior years of high school. A large focus of any subject in IB is the inclusion of learning from a global perspective. IB truly incorporates the best practices of learning styles and methodologies from as many cultures as possible into each of their subject areas. It is also very natural when working on an IB focused project to integrate multiple content areas. The projects (or dance concerts) that my students and I developed over a fifteen year time frame incorporated learning strategies from all the content areas that I just mentioned in the illustration in the Content Areas section. Also, the titles of each project are names I chose to avoid any copyright issues. Feel free to use the titles I came up with if you decide you'd like to incorporate one of these projects into your instruction. Last, I used dance and a bit of drama as my primary arts content areas, feel free to blend and mash-up any artistic discipline. These projects are broad enough that any artistic practice will work for telling the stories.

THE FORMAT

Just to give you an overall understanding of the format and time frame, my students and I spent an entire school year immersed in each project. The theme was decided by the junior students(who would be seniors the next school year). The "script" was written at the end of the spring semester so I would have time over the summer to develop the curriculum for the year, as well as schedule guest artists to do workshops on dance styles, and residencies to choreograph certain solo pieces. During the school year the students would dive into researching historical/cultural content of their assigned "scenes" from the script. Once research was completed, classes with the guest artists would take place, then the students would begin choreographing their dances using movement ideas taught in the guest artist's classes. They also began developing their overall artistic vision of how their dance would look onstage, with costumes, make-up, set pieces, etc. Once that part of the process was complete, the students auditioned additional dancers to be in their group pieces. The IB dance students were expected to take a leadership role in teaching their dancers choreography, collecting the costumes, and collaborating with the other IB dancers to tie all the dance pieces together for the entire production, which created a sort of "ballet" that depicted the storyline from all the dance numbers. I took on the role of "producer" making sure the students had a structure (rehearsal schedules) for the overall project; they had set boundaries and class policies for appropriate etiquette of working together as "pre-professional" artists; they had small budgets that each group managed for costumes, props, or set pieces; and even though they took artistic control of their own dances, I had final say about the overall direction of the project. In other words, I was the boss. Each IB dance student was expected to work through and document the creative process of developing their dance pieces. They had journaling assignments throughout the year for documenting their work. Yes, it was a huge project, and a lot of pieces to manage, but at the end of the production my students loved what they created and gained such a wealth of knowledge not only about a new culture, but the Creative Process and how to use it for creating dance pieces for a large production. The dances and excerpts of their written work were submitted to IB for assessments at the end of the year.

THE PROJECTS

Dunsinane Hill – This was the first themed project that we developed at the beginning of the IB dance pilot. We decided to start with "what we knew" for the first year. The students read and researched Shakespeare's _Macbeth_, studying dance traditions from the British Isles. The students then wrote a script that detailed how each dance (either solo, duet, or small group) piece would convey the story of Macbeth. (You can choose any Shakespeare play to adapt.)

- Content areas that were integrated into this project were: History, Language Arts, Dance, Drama, Music

Sensei Taro – For our second year we decided to step out of our comfort zone and learn about a culture very different from ours. _Sensei Taro_ was the adaptation of the children's play _The Honorable Urishima Taro_. The dancers researched, studied, and incorporated dance traditions from Japan. This play can be found through Dramatic Publishing at: www.dramaticpublishing.com. You can also purchase the script from Amazon. The same format that I describe above was used for this project.

- Content areas that were integrated into this project were: History, Language Arts, Science, Dance, Drama, Music, Visual Arts

The Dreamcatcher – was an adaptation of Paulo Coehlo's book _The Alchemist_. The focus of study was on Afro-Brazilian dance traditions. Coehlo's book can be found through Amazon or most book stores.

- Content areas that were integrated into this project were: History, Language Arts, Math, Science, Dance, Music, Visual Arts

Cinduri – was an Indian adaptation of the story of Cinderella. The students studied and learned dance traditions from India. The story was adapted from a children's book called _Anklet for a Princess_. I found multiple copies of the book on Amazon.

- Content areas that were integrated into this project were: History, Math, Science, Dance, Drama, Music, Visual Arts

Walkabout – was an adaptation of the creation stories from the Australian Aboriginal people. Students studied indigenous dance traditions from Australia. I found the creation stories in a book called _Gadi Mirrabooka: Australian Aboriginal Tales from the Dreaming_. I found the book at our local library, but also found copies on Amazon.

- Content areas that were integrated into this project were: History, Math, Science, Dance, Drama, Music, Visual Arts

JourneyMan – was the adaptation of _Gulliver's Travels_. The students researched multiple cultures in this project. They studied African, Polynesian, Chinese, and Russian Cossack dance traditions. _Gulliver's Travels_ should be easy to find from multiple sources. There might even be a copy in your school's library.

- Content areas that were integrated into this project were: History, Language Arts, Science, Dance, Media Arts, Music

Mami Wata – was an adaptation of Caribbean folktales that focus on the mermaid myths. Afro-Caribbean dance traditions, Capoeira & Katherine Dunham technique was researched and studied. I did an online search for "mermaid myths" and came up with multiple websites that have many different stories about mermaids. The words Mami Wata literally mean Mammy Water, which is the name of the water deity in many of the mermaid tales from the Caribbean and Africa.

- Content areas that were integrated into this project were: History, Science, Dance, Media Arts, Music

Firedance – the Plains Tribes from the Native American culture were researched and studied using tribal creation stories that were depicted through dance and movement. For this particular project I collaborated with a local dance company who performed with my students. A large focus on the theme of this project was on the "unity of community" and the generational respect the Native American culture has for all members of their community. The students did an online search for the tribal creation stories of the Plains

Indians and collected many different sources from many different tribes.

- Content areas that were integrated into this project were: History, Dance, Music, Visual Arts

Pandora's Odyssey – focused on selected stories from Greek Mythology, as well as researching and learning traditional Greek folk dance and traditions. The Greek myths are easy to find from any online source, as well as most libraries.

- Content areas that were integrated into this project were: History, Language Arts, Dance, Drama, Music

IB GRIMM - based on *Grimm's Fairytales*, with a contemporary twist. Research was conducted of German choreographer Pina Bausch, as well as the contemporary music scene in Berlin. Any Grimm's fairytale will work for this project. Grimm's fairytales are easy to find online or at any bookstore, or library.

- Content areas that were integrated into this project were: History, Language Arts, Science, Dance, Drama, Media Arts, Music

A FINAL NOTE ABOUT THEMED, CULTURAL PROJECTS

Every culture has utilized masks at some point in their artistic history. Every culture has built puppets and used them for storytelling. Most cultures have made quilts that are beautiful works of art. As well as many cultures have developed amazing <u>mosaic art</u> pieces. Any mask, puppet, quilt, or mosaic will highly likely not only have traditional stories behind how, or why, it was designed, but any of those pieces of art have mathematical, scientific, and historical aspects that can be taught. For instance, how much mathematical knowledge does it take to make a quilt or a puppet? How much science and math is included in making mosaic tiles and art? What is the history of the masks that were used in any Greek drama, or African tribal ceremony? There is a wealth of arts integration that can be applied just by studying the origins of masks and puppetry from each culture. Have your students not only make a mask or puppet, as you share the historical, mathematical or scientific concepts that coincide with the art form, but then let them play with what they made and turn it into a performance. We sold tickets to all our performances. The annual IB dance concert became a very popular fund-raiser for my program.

Technical theatre projects are rich with mathematical, scientific, and visual arts concepts. With all the technology that is used today in a theatre production, the use of media arts has become very popular. The last three to four of my dance concerts incorporated a large screen behind the dancers that could either project a location, or could include a slide show, or short video of artistic shapes looping during the performance. So, if there are any set pieces, costumes, lighting, video, or sound aspects to your project, instruction for technical theatre incorporates a ton of arts integration.

Finding music for dance can be a challenge, especially when you are looking for up tempo, cultural music without lyrics. Instrumental music is the best music to use for these types of projects, unless you are incorporating live instrumental or vocal music selections that the students are performing. Otherwise, it can be hard to find more contemporary sounding music that has a good beat, or that matches the storyline. I have found that the music composed for movie soundtracks works really well, just try to steer away from well-known tracks that have iconic attachments to them, like the theme to the movie *Titanic*. I also came across a couple of styles of music called *Acid Jazz*, or *Chillout* while on my trips to the UK for IB dance meetings. I would spend hours searching around iTunes for *Chillout* CD tracks from the culture of the theme that we were studying at the time. For instance, when we developed *Cinduri*, I searched for *Indian Chillout*. There are hundreds of CD's with literally thousands of songs that are upbeat, contemporary, instrumental, appropriate music to purchase and download. If you don't have a budget to buy music, then go over to YouTube and do your search there. Nine times out of ten, if you find a song that you liked in iTunes, there will be a YouTube version. The YouTube version is usually free.

We also cannot forget <u>food</u>! Food is great addition to any cultural project. I always tried to incorporate food into any lesson, unit or large cultural project that I did with my students. There is a lot of learning that can happen when you include food. Not only does food bring people together in a unique way, but it truly helps us to understand all aspects of any culture. So as you begin to explore arts integrated cultural projects, don't forget the food. You can sell culturally themed concessions at your performances, you can have a cultural "potluck" day in class where the students bring a dish and everyone shares the history of where it came from and why it was created. The ideas are endless when it comes to food. If your school community is diverse, it might be fun to have parents from each culture make their favorite dish and bring it to share in class one day. Ask them to share stories of traditions from their culture while everyone samples the food. (Many times as children growing up in their native country, the parents learned traditional folk dances. So ask them to share a dance if they grew up dancing.) However you incorporate the aspect of food, it will open the door for a fun way to experience different cultures. Everyone loves to eat!

The Assessment Cake

Arts education is a core academic subject
and an essential element of a complete and
balanced education for all students.
—Anonymous

IN THIS SECTION

This section is designed to coincide with and assess any of the activities, exercises or themed projects in this book. Each rubric can be used in multiple classroom, rehearsal, or workshop situations. All rubrics were developed by either my mentor and colleague Dr. Denina Brown, my colleagues at the Colorado Department of Education, or myself. They easily align with national or state arts standards. The rubrics also assess Essential Life Skills (also known as 21st century skills) that are discussed throughout this book.

When Dr. Brown and I first began developing these rubrics, we decided that if we were designing rubrics for a book that discusses Creative Process, our rubrics needed to look creative in their design. So just as Bloom devised his Taxonomy of Learning in a triangle shape, Dr. Brown and I decided to turn Bloom's triangle upside down to show the depth of learning when assessing Creativity. Then we decided to step "outside of the box" to create the Composition Rubric. For the Performance Rubric we included a spiral mix of simple and expressive descriptors to assess student performances. Last, but not least, we developed a student assessment tool that allows each student to reflect on and assess their own Creative Process in the Evaluation Rubric, which illustrates the "rock star" qualities that we all know our students embody. Each of these four rubrics can also be used by the students to assess their creativity, compositional skills, performance, or evaluate their process. These rubrics are not only for the teachers, the students can use them as well.

Along with those four rubrics, I also included a sample of a traditional rubric template that uses a few descriptors from my Creativity, Composition and Performance Rubrics. This template illustrates how the descriptors can be creatively gathered from each rubric and tailored for any lesson, or project. There is no right or wrong way to mix or match the descriptors from any of these rubrics. Have fun deciding which areas you want to assess your students, and how you will develop your own creative rubrics. I also included a blank rubric template at the end of this section designed for you to jot down and structure your own ideas and descriptors for assessing your students. Enjoy giving one of the most important pieces of the Creative Process to your students... constructive feedback!

1) Commits to brainstorming effectively – 5

2) Communicates ideas with details – 5

3) Collaborates effectively – 5

4) Utilizes synthesis – 5

5) Visualizes a goal/develops a plan – 5

6) Perceives similarities & differences – 5

7) Creates metaphor (tolerates ambiguity) – 10

8) Links ideas/concepts to a progression – 10

9) Blends 2-4 components. Ex: thoughts, objects, sounds, colors, words – 15

10) Explores solutions to problems when developing final product(s) – 5

11) Discovers relationships with contrasting items. – 5

12) Incorporates a specific style for a specific reason – 10

13) Finds a novel result – 15

Developed by Dr. Denina Brown

Total Score: _ _ _ _ _ _ _ _ /100

Creativity Rubric

1) Utilizes a process for exploration/discovery (Ex: Improvisation) - 10

2) Consistent technique, structure/form was used to craft or arrange segments/sequences - 15

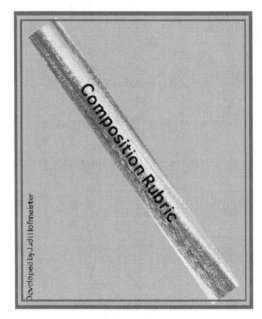

7) Develops a system for refining and revision - 10

8) Overall meaning/message of piece is well defined and easy to understand - 20

Composition Rubric

Developed by Judi Hofmeister

3) Each segment/sequence flows well into the next - 10

4) Unique and imaginative ideas are present in the composition - 15

5) Applies appropriate compositional elements (space, time, dynamics, melody/harmony) - 10

6) Overall piece consists of a strong beginning, middle and ending - 10

Total Score: _ _ _ _ _ _ _ _ /100

Developed by
Judi Hofmeister

Performance Rubric

Total Score: _ _ _ _ _ _ _ _ /100

3) Exceptional interpretation/expression of performance - 15

4) Consistent flow of performance - 10

7) Overall dynamic impact - 15

5) Solid memorization of material - 10

2) Outstanding technical proficiency - 15

6) Strong beginning, middle and ending of the performance - 15

1) Distinct confidence during performance - 20

Student Evaluation Rubric

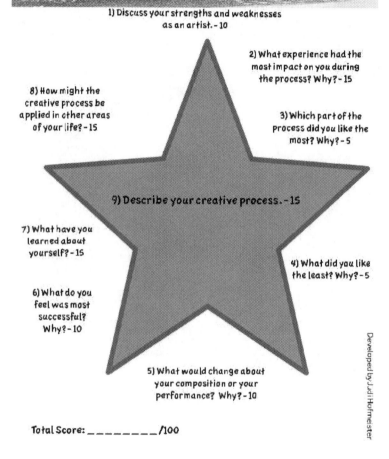

1) Discuss your strengths and weaknesses as an artist. - 10

2) What experience had the most impact on you during the process? Why? - 15

8) How might the creative process be applied in other areas of your life? - 15

3) Which part of the process did you like the most? Why? - 5

9) Describe your creative process. - 15

7) What have you learned about yourself? - 15

4) What did you like the least? Why? - 5

6) What do you feel was most successful? Why? - 10

5) What would change about your composition or your performance? Why? - 10

Total Score: _ _ _ _ _ _ _ _ /100

Developed by Judi Hofmeister

RUBRIC: SAMPLE

Concepts and skills students master: *Understanding of the Creative Process*
Content Areas: *Arts Integration*
Standards and Grade Level Expectations: *Any grade level can be applied*

Level of Mastery	Above Mastery	Mastery of Grade Level Standards	Approaching Mastery	Novice
Scoring Criteria	10 Exceeds expectations	8 Successful understanding	6 Moderate understanding	4 Little understanding
Brainstormed effectively				
Explored solutions to problems for final product				
Blended components				
(contents & methods)				
Utilized creative process				
Shared unique ideas				
Developed a system to refine & revise				
(rehearsal process)				

Strong beginning, middle & end			
Smooth flow of performance & transitions between stories			
Utilized interpretive expression for performance			
Meaning of story was well defined & easy to understand			

TOTAL POINTS_____

EMPTY RUBRIC TEMPLATE

Concepts and skills students master:

Content Areas:

Standards and Grade Level Expectations:

Level of Mastery	Above Mastery	Mastery of Grade Level Standards	Approaching Mastery	Novice
Scoring Criteria	10 Exceeds expectations	8 Successful understanding	6 Moderate understanding	4 Little understanding

TOTAL POINTS _____

A FINAL DISCUSSION ABOUT CREATIVE PROCESS

Everything is process: even a rock slowly changes ... or when a beautiful new bit of order emerges from what was more or less chaotic. Like a cake being baked from a bunch of ingredients, plus heat and water.—Peter Harris

My students have heard me ask over and over again, "In what other areas of your life can you use the creative process?" It's a thought-provoking question for them, and during one class a student popped up and said, "Everywhere!" Exactly! The creative process can be used in every facet of our lives. The process teaches Essential Life Skills that can be used every day:

1. Working collaboratively within a group—one of the most important skills one can learn.
2. Making decisions—this is a skill that a lot of my students really struggle with. Why? Why can it be such a challenge to simply make a decision? I encourage you to help guide your students in decision-making processes.
3. Listening to each other—a skill that seems to make most of my high-school students very uncomfortable. It's the simple art of listening to your surroundings, to what another person has to say, to the music, and to your cue from your scene partner. Oftentimes we are in such a hurry that we don't slow down and listen to what is happening in the moment; we don't connect, and we miss a lot of important information.

I encourage you to find a couple quick and simple listening exercises that you can do at the beginning or the ending of each class period.

4. Creative Problem-solving—thinking outside of the box, dancing on the other side of the barre. The arts encourage us to do just that and then apply it to the art form. I ask my students to also apply it to their everyday lives.

Quite a lot of research has been done into and about the Creative Process. Corporations, educational institutions, scientists, and architects have looked into the creative process for new and innovative ways not only to create art but also to improve leadership skills and sales that generate greater economic benefits. As a matter of fact, many large corporations actually require employees to go through basic "creativity training." It is believed that if employees actually realize and believe they are creative, they will collaborate in a more expressive way and not be as hesitant to use their imaginations in organizational situations.

The creative work that is done in arts education has an overwhelming outreach beyond just being involved in your typical high-school play. Arts education and the creative process encourage us to look at the "big picture," to be more global-minded and not fear being entrepreneurial, trendsetting or ahead of the game in a world that is technologically moving at the speed of light ... or faster! When my students ask me why the work we're doing in my class is important, I tell them performing arts is a three-dimensional art form. We embody the art. There is no other species on this planet that creates like we do. To be creative is the highest-level of thinking and learning we do as humans. To be creative takes everything we learn in our core academic classes and applies that knowledge to something meaningful and beautiful—a living, breathing art form. In my book, it doesn't get any better than that!

Creativity is contagious, pass it on! --Einstein

RESOURCES

Aguilar, C., Goodwin, D., Hofmeister, J., "High Impact Instructional Arts Strategies." District Sample Curriculum Project. Colorado Department of Education. 2016. www.cde.state.co.us/standardsandinstruction/highimpactinstructionalstrategies

Belt, Linda, and Rebecca Stockley. 1991. *Improvisation through Theatre Sports.* Seattle, WA: Thespis Productions.

Cameron, Julia. 2002. *The Artist's Way: A Spiritual Path to Higher Creativity.* New York: Penguin Putnam Inc.

Covey, Stephen R. 1989, 2004. The Seven Habits of Highly Effective People. New York: Free Press.

Cunningham, Merce. 2009. *Chance Dance Choreography Workshop.* New York: NDEO.

Epstein, Robert. 2000. *The Big Book of Creativity Games.* New York: McGraw-Hill.

Ghiselin, Brewster. 1985. *The Creative Process: A Symposium.* Berkeley, CA: University of California Press.

Harris, Peter. 2011, 2012. *How to Be Creative—A Passport to Creativity: The Beauty of New Ideas.* New Zealand: Eutopia Press.

Mallen, A. H. 2000. *Dance G. C. S. Easy: Space, Actions, Dynamics, Relationships: The Teacher Resource.* Bradford, BD: Dance in Education Services.

Minton, Sandra Cerny. 1997. *Choreography: A Basic Approach Using Improvisation.* Champagne, IL: Human Kinetics.

Pink, Daniel H. 2005, 2006. *A Whole New Mind: Why Right-Brainers Will Rule the Future.* New York: Riverhead Books.

Root-Bernstein, Robert, and Michele. 2001. *Sparks of Genius: The Thirteen Thinking Tools of the World's Most Creative People*. New York: Houghton Mifflin Company.

Spolin, V. 1986. *Theater Games for the Classroom: A Teacher's Handbook*. Evanston, IL: Northwestern University Press.

Tharp, Twyla, and Mark Reiter. 2003. *The Creative Habit—Learn It and Use It for Life: A Practical Guide*. New York: Simon & Schuster.

Zaporah, Ruth. 1995. *Action Theatre: The Improvisation of Presence*. Berkeley, CA: North Atlantic Books.

DANCE, THEATRE, AND MUSIC SUGGESTIONS

THE DANCE CAKE

Suggestions for Shapes for the exercise *Shape, Shape & Reshape*

- Heart
- Star
- Arrow
- Spiral
- Diamond
- Triangle
- Square
- Circle
- Crescent Moon

Suggestions for *Elements of Nature* exercise:

- Tumbleweed
- Candle flame (any sized fire will work)
- Blooming flower
- Tree
- Leaf in the wind
- Pinecone
- Lightening
- Rain
- Ocean waves
- Gentle stream

Suggestions for *Emotions Dance*
(this list can be used for the theatre games as well)

- Hurried
- Surprised
- Confused
- Bored
- Frustrated
- Overwhelmed
- Embarrassed
- Nervous
- Shocked
- Silly
- Worried

THE THEATRE CAKE

Suggestions of Tasks for *Sports Caster*, or *What R U Doing?*

- Mowing the lawn
- Dusting the furniture
- Washing the dishes
- Painting the house
- Trimming the hedges
- Washing the car
- Vacuuming the stairs
- Cooking breakfast
- Chopping vegetables
- Grating cheese
- Cleaning the toilet
- Sweeping the garage

Suggestions for Interesting Situations for *Stop/Freeze*

- Filling jars at a pickle factory
- Pushing a stalled car uphill
- Getting stuck in a full elevator
- Sitting on the freeway
- Late to work and missed the bus
- Standing in line for concert tickets
- Waiting for a doctor's appointment
- On the deck of a ship in a storm
- Climbing a mountain
- Swimming in the ocean with sharks
- Sunbathing at the beach at night
- Herding cattle

Suggestions of Vacation Spots for *Slide Show*

- The pyramids
- The great wall of China
- The Australian Outback
- An African Safari
- Skiing the Matterhorn
- The Grand Canyon
- Hawaii
- Antarctica
- A Viking ship
- The Roman Colosseum
- Pompeii
- The moon

THE VOCAL CAKE

Big Band/USO song suggestions

- "Sentimental Journey"
- "Boogie Woogie Bugle Boy"
- "Don't Sit under the Apple Tree"
- "Bei Mir Bist Du Schoen"
- "Bandstand Boogie"
- "Stray Cat Strut"
- "Tuxedo Junction"
- "A Nightingale Sang in Berkeley Square"
- "Java Jive"
- "Operator"

Nifty '50s/'60s song suggestions

- "Greased Lightning"
- "We Go Together"
- "Up, Up and Away"
- "Downtown"
- "Serve Yourself" (from *Pump Boys and Dinettes*)
- "Farmer Tan" (from *Pump Boys and Dinettes*)
- "Earth Angel"
- "Sounds of Silence"
- "Rock around the Clock"
- "Please Mr. Postman"

Madrigal Dinner suggested resources for Madrigals

- *The Oxford Book of English Madrigals* by Philip Lane Ledger, SATB a cappella

- *The Complete Madrigal Dinner Booke* by Paul Brandvik

Victorian Caroling suggested resource for carols

- *Christmas in Song,* arranged by Theodore Preuss, SATB

ABOUT THE AUTHOR

Judi Hofmeister was hired at Douglas County High School in Castle Rock, Colorado in 1993 after leaving a ten-year professional performing-arts career. For twenty years Miss Hofmeister taught theatre, dance, vocal music, and sat as chair of the performing-arts department. In 2000, Judi was selected as the only Colorado public-school dance teacher to help develop and pilot the International Baccalaureate (IB) dance program. Her work on the IB Dance curriculum required multiple trips abroad to Cardiff, Wales and The Hague, Netherlands to collaborate with curriculum specialists and dance teachers from various countries. For fifteen years her IB Dance program was the only one of its kind in the state of Colorado.

Judi was awarded Dance Educator for 2009 by the Colorado Dance Alliance (CDA), and is the past president and a founding member of the Colorado Dance Education Organization (CoDEO). She currently is the Dance/Drama and Theatre Arts Consultant for the Colorado Department of Education (CDE) where she facilitates the development of standards, and curriculum for dance and theatre teachers throughout the state. Judi attended Loretto Heights College, the University of Denver, and Regis University.

Judi is available for large or small group professional development seminars or workshops, arts integration consultation, or development of performing arts standards, curriculum and assessments. Please visit Judi at: www.h2ohproductions.com

Printed in the United States
By Bookmasters